ESG Investing Uncovered: Myths, Truths, and the Billion-Dollar Opportunity

How Sustainability is Reshaping Markets

Subarna Poddar

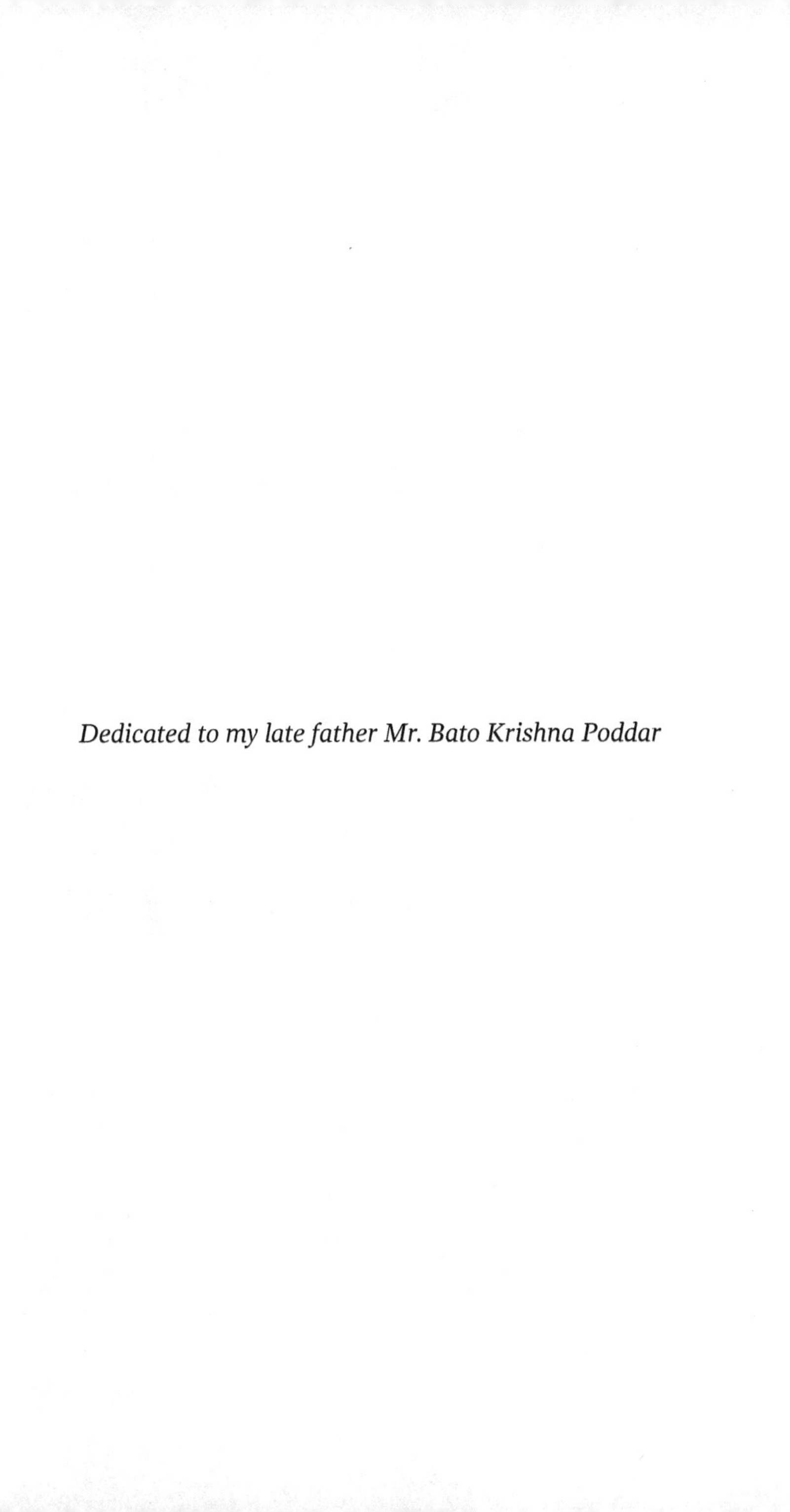

Dedicated to my late father Mr. Bato Krishna Poddar

Acknowledgments

Writing this book has been both a personal and professional journey, deeply shaped by the values of my late father, Bato Krishna Poddar. His commitment to responsible stewardship and ethical leadership instilled in me a profound appreciation for sustainable and impactful investing. Our evening conversations, where he stressed the importance of aligning financial goals with societal well-being, sparked my passion for Environmental, Social, and Governance (ESG) investments.

To my mother, Sima Poddar—your resilience and dedication have been a guiding force. Your unwavering commitment to family and community has exemplified the essence of social responsibility. My sisters, Satadipa and Samprita Poddar, and my brother-in-law, Rahul Majumdar— your insightful perspectives and steadfast support have deepened my understanding of governance and ethical decision-making.

A heartfelt acknowledgment to my longtime friend, Anuj Shinde. Your intellectual curiosity, deep knowledge of financial markets, and relentless passion for sustainability have made an indelible impact on this book. Our extensive discussions—ranging from ESG frameworks to the future of impact investing—have challenged my perspectives and refined my thoughts. Your ability to dissect complex financial principles and translate them into meaningful insights has been invaluable. Beyond the intellectual exchanges, your unwavering support and encouragement have been a steady source of motivation throughout this journey.

To my mentors—your guidance and wisdom have played a crucial role in shaping my understanding of finance, ethics, and responsible investing. Your invaluable advice, whether through structured lessons or candid conversations, has provided clarity and direction in navigating complex financial landscapes. The lessons you have imparted extend beyond technical knowledge, fostering a mindset of integrity, diligence, and purpose. I am deeply grateful for your belief in my vision and for inspiring me to push the boundaries of sustainable finance.

To my family, friends, and colleagues—your diverse perspectives and support have enriched this journey, providing invaluable insights into the evolving landscape of ESG investments.

A special thanks to Notion Press for publishing this book and helping bring my vision to a wider audience. Their professionalism, expertise, and dedication to the publishing process have been instrumental in shaping the final work. From editing to design and distribution, their support has ensured that this book reaches those eager to explore the world of sustainable and responsible investing.

Synopsis

Environmental, Social, and Governance (ESG) investing has skyrocketed into a **$50 trillion market**, reshaping global finance. While some view it as a game-changer for sustainability, others see it as an overhyped trend plagued by greenwashing and misleading claims. **Is ESG truly driving meaningful change, or is it just another marketing buzzword?** This book cuts through the noise to uncover the truth.

What This Book Explores:

- **How ESG ratings work—and why they often fail to measure real sustainability**
    - ◊ Unpacking the flaws in rating methodologies
    - ◊ Exposing inconsistencies and biases in ESG scoring systems
- **The greenwashing dilemma—how companies mislead investors**
    - ◊ Tactics used by corporations to appear more sustainable than they are
    - ◊ High-profile cases of ESG failures and misleading claims
- **The real winners and losers in ESG investing**
    - ◊ Who is genuinely driving change vs. who is capitalizing on the trend
    - ◊ Industry breakdowns: which sectors are thriving in ESG and which are falling behind
- **The future of ESG investing—what's next?**
    - ◊ How AI, big data, and new regulations will transform ESG investing

◊ The role of governments and financial institutions in enforcing transparency

- **How to identify authentic ESG opportunities**

  ◊ Key indicators to spot truly sustainable investments

  ◊ Strategies to avoid greenwashing traps and make informed decisions

Why Read This Book?

Featuring **in-depth case studies, expert insights, and actionable strategies**, this book is an essential guide for:

- **Investors** looking to maximize returns while making a positive impact

- **Finance professionals** seeking clarity in an increasingly complex ESG landscape

- **Corporate leaders** aiming to align business strategies with sustainability goals

- **Anyone passionate about responsible investing and the future of sustainable finance**

This book doesn't just explore ESG investing—it equips you with the knowledge to **separate hype from reality and invest with confidence in a rapidly evolving financial landscape.**

Contents

CHAPTER 1

The ESG Gold Rush or a Fool's Game?

Introduction: The Rise of ESG Investing

Over the past decade, Environmental, Social, and Governance (ESG) investing has evolved from a niche ethical movement into a dominant financial force. With assets projected to surpass $50 trillion by 2025, ESG has become a cornerstone of global capital markets. Yet, as billions pour into ESG funds, a critical question remains: Is ESG genuinely transforming finance, or is it merely a passing trend driven by marketing strategies and political agendas?

A Brief History of ESG Investing

The roots of ESG investing trace back to the 1970s, when Socially Responsible Investing (SRI) emerged, primarily focusing on excluding "sin stocks"—such as tobacco, alcohol, and weapons. Over time, investors shifted toward a more comprehensive approach that integrates environmental, social, and governance factors into financial decision-making. In 2006, the United Nations launched the Principles for Responsible Investment (PRI), encouraging institutional investors to incorporate ESG considerations into their analyses—a movement that has since gained significant momentum.

Why ESG Investing Is Booming

Four key drivers have fueled ESG's rapid expansion:

- **Investor Demand for Sustainability** – Younger generations, set to inherit over $30 trillion in wealth, increasingly prioritize investments that align with their ethical values.

- **Regulatory Pressure** – New disclosure requirements from the European Union and proposed regulations from the U.S. Securities and Exchange Commission (SEC) aim to curb greenwashing and enhance transparency.

- **Financial Benefits** – Studies suggest that companies with strong ESG practices often manage risk more effectively and may deliver superior long-term financial performance.

- **The Climate Crisis and Social Responsibility** – As climate disasters escalate, corporate accountability has become imperative, driving businesses toward more sustainable practices.

Challenges and Criticisms

Despite its potential, ESG investing faces several significant challenges:

- **Inconsistent ESG Ratings** – The lack of standardized methodologies among rating agencies leads to conflicting ESG scores, creating confusion for investors.

- **Performance Concerns** – While some ESG funds outperform traditional investments, others underperform and may carry higher fees.

- **Greenwashing** – Many companies market themselves as ESG-compliant without making meaningful changes, misleading investors.

Case Study: Tesla's ESG Downgrade

Tesla, once hailed as a sustainability leader, was removed from major ESG indices due to governance issues and labor controversies—while traditional energy companies retained their positions. This paradox highlights the flaws in ESG scoring systems and underscores the importance of thorough due diligence in evaluating ESG claims.

Author's Perspective

The ESG movement presents both opportunities and challenges. While integrating ESG factors can contribute to more resilient, long-term investments, the lack of standardized metrics and the prevalence of greenwashing mean investors must critically assess each claim. ESG is here to stay, but only those who dig deeper and scrutinize beyond the surface will truly capitalize on its potential.

CHAPTER 2

A Practical ESG Investment Framework – A Step-by-Step Guide

Introduction

For investors looking to align their portfolios with sustainable values, a structured approach is essential. This chapter provides a step-by-step framework to effectively integrate ESG factors into your investment strategy with clarity and confidence.

Step 1: Define Your ESG Objectives

- **Clarify Your Goals** – Determine whether your primary objective is long-term financial returns, positive social impact, or a balance of both.

- **Identify Focus Areas** – Decide whether to adopt a broad ESG strategy or target specific issues such as climate action, gender diversity, or corporate governance.

Step 2: Identify Reliable ESG Data Sources

- **Third-Party Ratings** – Leverage ratings from MSCI ESG Ratings, Sustainalytics, FTSE Russell, and S&P ESG scores to assess companies and funds.

- **Company Disclosures** – Review sustainability reports, SEC filings, and corporate responsibility statements for transparency and accountability.

- **Independent Research** – Consult studies and reports from NGOs and regulatory bodies to gain unbiased insights.

Step 3: Evaluate ESG Funds and Stocks

- **Analyze Holdings** – Ensure that a fund's portfolio aligns with your ESG criteria by avoiding companies with weak sustainability practices.

- **Assess Performance Metrics** – Compare ESG funds against traditional benchmarks to evaluate long-term performance potential.

- **Consider Expenses** – Weigh the costs of ESG funds and determine whether higher fees are justified by the added benefits.

Step 4: Diversify Your ESG Exposure

- **Expand Across Asset Classes** – Invest in a variety of asset types, including green bonds, impact investments, and sustainable real estate, to mitigate risk and enhance portfolio resilience.

Step 5: Engage in Active Ownership

- **Exercise Shareholder Rights** – Use your voting power to advocate for stronger ESG policies within companies.

- **Collaborate with Investors** – Join coalitions of like-minded investors to amplify influence on corporate ESG practices.

Investor Takeaway

A structured ESG investment approach—grounded in clear objectives, verified data, and proactive engagement—can drive both financial success and meaningful impact. By following this framework, investors can build sustainable, high-performing portfolios that align with their values and long-term goals.

CHAPTER 3

The ESG Boom—Hype or Reality?

A Brief History of ESG Investing

ESG investing did not emerge overnight. Its origins trace back to the 1970s when Socially Responsible Investing (SRI) focused on excluding "sin stocks" such as tobacco, alcohol, and weapons. Over time, investors moved beyond simply avoiding harmful industries to actively incorporating environmental, social, and governance factors into their investment analyses.

A pivotal moment came in 2006 with the launch of the **United Nations' Principles for Responsible Investment (PRI)**, which encouraged institutional investors to systematically integrate ESG criteria. Today, ESG is deeply embedded in global finance, with trillions of dollars managed under ESG mandates.

Why ESG Is Booming: Regulations, Investor Demand, and Risk Mitigation

Several key factors have fueled the rapid growth of ESG investing:

- **Regulatory Pressure** – Governments and regulatory bodies worldwide are imposing stricter sustainability disclosure requirements. For example, **Europe's Sustainable Finance Disclosure Regulation (SFDR)** mandates that asset managers disclose the environmental and social impact of their portfolios, while proposed **U.S. SEC regulations** aim to enhance ESG transparency with standardized, verifiable data.

- **Investor Demand** – Millennials and Gen Z, poised to inherit vast wealth, increasingly prioritize sustainability in their investment choices. Surveys indicate that many investors seek portfolios that align with their ethical values, pushing traditional asset managers to incorporate ESG factors into their strategies.

- **Risk Mitigation** – Companies with strong ESG practices are often better positioned to manage long-term risks, including regulatory shifts, climate-related disruptions, and reputational damage. Studies suggest that firms with robust ESG profiles tend to experience lower volatility during market downturns, making ESG investing a valuable risk management strategy.

ESG Fund Performance: Does It Really Outperform?

The performance of ESG funds remains a topic of debate. While proponents argue that sustainable investing delivers superior long-term returns, the reality is more nuanced:

- **Long-Term Resilience** – Research suggests that companies with strong ESG practices tend to be more resilient in the face of economic and environmental challenges. However, short-term performance varies, as ESG funds may carry higher expense ratios and often exclude high-performing sectors like fossil fuels.

- **Risk-Adjusted Returns** – ESG investing is more about **managing risk effectively** than guaranteeing outperformance. Investors may not always see dramatic alpha compared to traditional funds, but they often benefit from reduced downside risk and enhanced long-term sustainability.

- **Data Inconsistencies** – A major challenge in assessing ESG fund performance is the **lack of standardized ESG ratings**. Different rating agencies use diverse methodologies, resulting in significant discrepancies in ESG scores for the same company.

This inconsistency makes direct fund comparisons difficult.

Case Study: Tesla's ESG Downgrade

Tesla, widely recognized as a leader in sustainable innovation, has revolutionized the auto industry with its electric vehicles and commitment to renewable energy. Yet, despite these achievements, Tesla has faced significant scrutiny from ESG rating agencies:

- **Governance Issues** – Concerns over workplace practices, board oversight, and executive decision-making have weighed on Tesla's governance score.

- **Inconsistent Ratings** – While some agencies rate Tesla highly for its environmental impact, others penalize it for social and governance shortcomings. This discrepancy highlights the broader challenge of inconsistent ESG evaluation methods.

- **Investor Implications** – Tesla's case underscores the importance of looking beyond headline ESG scores. Investors must conduct thorough due diligence rather than relying solely on aggregated ratings.

Author's Perspective on the ESG Boom

The rapid rise of ESG investing is both promising and complex. While sustainable practices can drive long-term value and enhance risk management, ESG as a field is still evolving. The lack of standardized metrics and the risk of **greenwashing** require investors to approach ESG with both optimism and caution.

The real promise of ESG does not lie in **guaranteed outperformance** but in its **potential to reshape how we assess and manage risk in the modern economy**. For investors who look beyond the hype and conduct rigorous analysis, ESG offers a transformative approach to sustainable wealth creation.

CHAPTER 4

The ESG Civil War—Champions vs. Critics

ESG Advocates vs. Skeptics: The Great Debate

The debate over ESG investing has grown increasingly polarized. Proponents view ESG as the future of responsible capitalism—an essential tool for mitigating long-term risks and fostering sustainable growth. Critics, however, argue that ESG is overhyped, politically driven, and, in some cases, detrimental to financial returns.

- **Advocates' Perspective** – Supporters assert that integrating sustainability into investment decisions drives positive environmental and social change while protecting against risks such as climate disasters, regulatory fines, and reputational damage. They argue that companies committed to ESG are better aligned with future market demands and long-term value creation.

- **Skeptics' Perspective** – Critics contend that ESG metrics are overly subjective and that greenwashing is widespread. They caution that an excessive focus on ESG may lead to the exclusion of profitable sectors—such as traditional energy—that remain vital to the global economy. Additionally, they argue that political and ideological biases can distort investment decisions.

Wall Street's Role in Promoting ESG

Wall Street has played a pivotal role in mainstreaming ESG investing:

- **Institutional Integration** – Firms like **BlackRock and Vanguard** have embedded ESG criteria into their investment strategies, frequently stating that "climate risk is investment risk."

- **Shareholder Engagement** – Many institutional investors leverage their voting rights to push companies toward stronger ESG practices, fostering greater corporate accountability.

- **Market Innovation** – The rise of ESG-themed **ETFs and mutual funds** has made sustainable investing more accessible. However, this growth has also sparked concerns about fund dilution and potential greenwashing.

Political and Ideological Backlash Against ESG Investing

ESG investing has become a highly charged political issue, with growing resistance from policymakers and industry leaders:

- **Political Opposition** – Some U.S. state governments argue that ESG investing imposes political agendas on financial markets. Critics claim that ESG funds **penalize traditional industries** by prioritizing "politically correct" investments over financial performance.

- **Ideological Divides** – Detractors believe ESG is being used to force social and environmental policies onto businesses, while supporters maintain that ESG aligns long-term business success with broader societal benefits.

- **Regulatory Uncertainty** – This ideological divide has led to a **fragmented regulatory landscape**, with ESG disclosure standards varying significantly across regions, adding complexity for investors.

Case Study: Texas vs. BlackRock – The ESG Pushback

A prominent example of political resistance to ESG investing is the clash between the state of **Texas and major asset managers** like **BlackRock**:

- **Texas' Stance** – Texas lawmakers have accused BlackRock of divesting from fossil fuel industries and **using ESG criteria to favor investments that align with progressive environmental policies**. They argue that such practices threaten the economic stability of energy-dependent states.

- **BlackRock's Response** – BlackRock defends its ESG approach by emphasizing the long-term risks associated with climate change and the necessity of sustainable investment strategies. CEO **Larry Fink** has repeatedly stated that ESG integration is essential for managing financial risk in a changing global economy.

- **Investor Implications** – This conflict illustrates how ESG investing can become entangled with political and regional interests, underscoring the need for investors to consider the broader geopolitical context when making ESG-related decisions.

Author's Perspective on the ESG Civil War

The ongoing debate between ESG advocates and skeptics is essential to refining the industry, improving transparency, and ensuring that sustainability claims are backed by concrete action. As an investor, it is crucial to:

- **Maintain a balanced perspective**, recognizing both the potential benefits and inherent risks of ESG investing.

- **Conduct thorough due diligence**, rather than relying solely on headline ESG ratings.

- **Stay informed** about evolving regulations and political developments that could impact ESG strategies.

Ultimately, the future of ESG investing will depend on the willingness of **investors, companies, and regulators** to engage in constructive debate and implement meaningful reforms. Only by addressing these challenges head-on can ESG investing transition from a divisive trend to a **credible and enduring tool for sustainable finance**.

CHAPTER 5

Greenwashing—The Dark Side of ESG

What Is Greenwashing?

Greenwashing is a deceptive practice in which companies **exaggerate or misrepresent** their commitment to sustainability. It is primarily a marketing tactic designed to create the illusion of environmental and social responsibility without implementing meaningful changes. Companies engaged in greenwashing often use **vague language, unverified claims, or selective disclosures** to appear more sustainable than they truly are.

How Companies Manipulate ESG Scores

Companies may manipulate ESG scores through several tactics:

- **Selective Disclosure** – Highlighting minor sustainability initiatives while ignoring significant environmental or social risks.

- **Misleading Labels and Certifications** – Using terms such as **"eco-friendly" or "sustainable"** without third-party validation.

- **Carbon Offsetting Loopholes** – Claiming carbon neutrality by purchasing offsets instead of reducing actual emissions.

- **Data Manipulation** – Adjusting self-reported metrics—altering measurement boundaries or using outdated data—to artificially improve ESG scores.

These tactics distort a company's true sustainability performance and undermine the credibility of ESG investing.

Major Greenwashing Scandals

Several high-profile cases have exposed the dark side of greenwashing:

- **Volkswagen's Dieselgate** – Once considered an environmentally responsible automaker, Volkswagen was found to have installed defeat devices in diesel engines to cheat emissions tests, revealing a stark contrast between its public image and actual practices.

- **H&M's "Conscious Collection"** – Marketed as sustainable, H&M's collection has faced criticism for continuing to rely on unsustainable production methods and labor exploitation.

- **Shell's Carbon Claims** – Despite aggressive marketing of its sustainability initiatives, investigations have revealed that much of Shell's **green branding** is based on carbon credits and token projects that do little to reduce overall emissions.

Regulatory Actions to Combat Greenwashing

To restore trust in ESG investing, regulators worldwide are implementing stricter policies:

- **Stricter Disclosure Requirements** – Agencies such as the **U.S. SEC** and the **European Union** now mandate verified ESG disclosures from companies.

- **Standardization Efforts** – Initiatives like the **EU's Green Taxonomy** and frameworks from the **International Sustainability Standards Board (ISSB)** aim to create uniform ESG reporting standards.

- **Legal and Financial Penalties** – Companies found guilty of greenwashing face increasing lawsuits and regulatory fines, serving as a deterrent against deceptive practices.

- **Enhanced Auditing and Third-Party Verification** – Independent audits are becoming more common to ensure ESG claims are backed by **accurate and reliable data.**

How Investors Can Identify Misleading ESG Claims

Investors seeking to avoid greenwashing should consider these strategies:

1. **Look Beyond the ESG Score** – Examine underlying data and methodologies rather than relying solely on headline ratings.

2. **Demand Transparency** – Choose companies that provide **comprehensive, verifiable** sustainability reports and undergo independent audits.

3. **Focus on Measurable Impact** – Prioritize firms that demonstrate **clear, quantifiable outcomes** (e.g., actual emission reductions, and improved labor conditions).

4. **Watch for Red Flags** – Be cautious of **vague sustainability claims, excessive reliance on carbon offsets**, or insufficient details on governance and social policies.

5. **Cross-Reference Multiple Sources** – Use various **ESG rating agencies and independent research** to gain a holistic view of a company's sustainability performance.

Author's Perspective on Greenwashing

Greenwashing remains one of the biggest challenges in ESG investing. While many companies have **genuinely embraced sustainable practices,** a significant number exploit ESG trends for **reputational and financial gain** without making real changes.

As regulators **tighten standards** and investors become more discerning, the future of ESG investing will depend on **transparency, accountability, and the ability to distinguish between genuine commitment and marketing spin.** True sustainability requires **concrete action—not just clever branding.**

CHAPTER 6

A Deep Dive into ESG Metrics and Ratings

How ESG Ratings Work and Why They Differ Across Agencies

ESG ratings aim to quantify a company's performance across environmental, social, and governance factors. However, the **lack of a universal standard** leads to significant variations among rating agencies.

The rating process typically begins with a review of a company's disclosures, including **sustainability reports, regulatory filings, and third-party audits**. Each agency applies its weighting to various ESG factors—some prioritize environmental impact, while others focus on governance or social issues.

These evaluations combine **quantitative data** (e.g., carbon emissions) with **qualitative assessments** (e.g., management practices), making ESG scoring inherently complex. To ensure fairness, sector-specific adjustments are often made to account for industry differences.

Comparing Major ESG Rating Agencies

Several key players dominate the ESG rating landscape:

- **MSCI ESG Ratings** – Assigns ratings from **AAA (industry leader) to CCC (laggard)** based on a company's exposure to industry-specific ESG risks and its ability to manage them.

- **Sustainalytics** – Focuses on a company's **ESG risk exposure and risk management effectiveness**, providing insights widely used by institutional investors.

- **FTSE Russell ESG Scores** – Evaluates companies across all three ESG dimensions, emphasizing **data comparability across industries and regions**.

- **S&P Global ESG Scores** – Utilizes a mix of **quantitative metrics and qualitative assessments**, drawing from sources such as the **Dow Jones Sustainability Index**.

Challenges of Self-Reported ESG Data

Reliance on **self-reported ESG data** presents several challenges:

- **Inconsistency** – Companies use different reporting standards and timeframes, leading to discrepancies.

- **Transparency Issues** – Without **independent verification**, the accuracy of ESG claims is difficult to assess.

- **Greenwashing Risk** – Some companies may **manipulate self-reported data** to present a more favorable ESG profile than reality.

Investor Guide: How to Use ESG Scores Effectively

To maximize the value of ESG ratings, investors should adopt a **critical and multi-faceted approach**:

1. **Utilize Multiple Ratings** – Rely on assessments from **various agencies** to develop a well-rounded perspective.

2. **Understand Methodologies** – Familiarize yourself with each agency's rating system and how it weighs different ESG factors.

3. **Analyze Trends Over Time** – Assess a company's **ESG performance trajectory**, rather than focusing solely on a single rating.

4. **Supplement with Independent Research** – Cross-reference ESG scores with **third-party reports, news sources, and direct company disclosures.**

5. **Integrate with Traditional Analysis** – Combine ESG insights with **conventional financial metrics** for more informed investment decisions.

Author's Perspective on ESG Metrics and Ratings

While ESG ratings are **valuable tools** for evaluating investments, they are not without flaws. The **lack of standardization and reliance on self-reported data** necessitate a **critical, multi-source approach** to ESG analysis.

By cross-referencing multiple ratings, conducting independent research, and integrating ESG insights with **traditional financial analysis**, investors can better **manage risk and identify long-term sustainable opportunities.**

CHAPTER 7

ESG Winners and Losers—Who's Walking the Talk?

Introduction: Separating Genuine Sustainability from Lip Service

With billions of dollars flowing into ESG investments, companies display varying levels of commitment to sustainability. Some are genuinely transforming their operations, while others enhance their image merely to attract capital. This chapter explores **which industries are leading the ESG transition, and which are falling behind,** and highlights a **case study on ESG misrepresentation** alongside an analysis of the **top 10 most sustainable companies poised to lead in 2025.**

Industries Leading the ESG Transition

Several sectors are **setting the standard for sustainability** by integrating ESG principles into their core strategies:

- **Renewable Energy** – Companies in **solar, wind, and hydropower** are reshaping the energy landscape. For instance, **Ørsted** has transitioned from a fossil fuel-based enterprise into a **global leader in offshore wind energy**, significantly reducing its carbon footprint.

- **Technology** – The tech sector is leveraging **innovation to cut emissions, enhance supply chain transparency, and drive sustainability initiatives.** A standout example is **Microsoft**, which has pledged to become **carbon-negative by 2030.**

- **Consumer Goods** – Brands are increasingly adopting **ethical sourcing, circular economy practices, and** waste reduction strategies. **Unilever**, for instance, has deeply integrated sustainability into its supply chain and product development, proving that **profitability and responsibility can coexist**.

Sectors Falling Behind

Despite ESG momentum, some industries continue to struggle with meaningful progress:

- **Fossil Fuels** – While some energy firms promote sustainability initiatives, the industry **remains one of the largest carbon emitters**, facing increasing regulatory and investor pressure.

- **Fast Fashion** – This sector is notorious for **high waste production, environmental degradation, and questionable labor practices**, making it a poor fit for long-term ESG goals.

- **Industrial Agriculture** – Large-scale farming practices often involve **deforestation, excessive water consumption, and pollution**, making substantial ESG improvements difficult without radical systemic change.

Case Study: The Sembcorp Coal Controversy

Once regarded as a leader in sustainable energy, **Sembcorp Industries** made headlines when it **sold off its coal assets—**a move seemingly in line with ESG principles. However, further investigation revealed that Sembcorp **transferred these assets to a subsidiary, allowing it to continue profiting from coal production**.

This case underscores the **risk of superficial ESG adjustments—**without a genuine commitment to decarbonization, such actions amount to mere **corporate rebranding rather than real change**.

The Top 10 Most Sustainable Companies of 2025

Based on **comprehensive ESG analysis**, the following companies stand out as **industry leaders in sustainability**:

1. **Ørsted** – A global renewable energy leader, drastically reducing emissions through wind and solar investments.

2. **Microsoft** – Committed to achieving **carbon negativity** and setting ethical AI governance standards.

3. **Tesla** – Despite governance challenges, remains a driving force behind **electric vehicle adoption and clean energy innovation**.

4. **Unilever** – A sustainability leader in the **consumer goods sector**, embedding ESG principles into its core business.

5. **IKEA** – Investing heavily in **circular economy initiatives and renewable energy** to lower its environmental footprint.

6. **Patagonia** – Recognized for **environmental activism and sustainable business practices**, setting a benchmark for corporate responsibility.

7. **Beyond Meat** – Innovating in the **plant-based food industry**, significantly reducing the environmental impact of traditional meat production.

8. **Nvidia** – Leading in **energy-efficient computing and responsible corporate governance**, key to the future of AI-driven sustainability.

9. **Schneider Electric** – Specializing in **energy management and smart grid solutions** for more sustainable power infrastructure.

10. **Autodesk** – Pioneering **sustainable design technology** in **architecture and construction**, reducing material waste and energy consumption.

Author's Perspective on ESG Winners and Losers

The contrast between **genuine ESG leaders and companies capitalizing on the sustainability trend** is clear. Investors must go beyond **marketing claims and surface-level ESG scores** to focus on **measurable impact and authentic corporate transformation**.

True ESG winners are those that **embed sustainability into their business models**—not just as a branding exercise, but as a **long-term strategic advantage**. This distinction is **critical for investors seeking to build a resilient, future-proof portfolio** in an increasingly sustainability-driven world.

CHAPTER 8

ESG in Emerging Markets—Challenges and Opportunities

Introduction: The Importance of ESG in Emerging Markets

Emerging markets represent a unique and underexplored frontier for ESG investing. While these economies face significant developmental challenges, they also offer vast opportunities for **sustainable growth.** In these regions, ESG practices are not just **risk management tools**—they are **critical drivers of long-term economic development and social progress.**

Why ESG Matters in Emerging Markets

Several factors make ESG integration essential in developing economies:

- **Climate Vulnerability** – Many emerging markets are disproportionately affected by environmental disruptions, making **sustainable practices essential for economic stability.**

- **Social Impact** – In regions struggling with **social inequality and labor issues,** strong ESG frameworks can drive meaningful improvements in **community well-being and workforce conditions.**

- **Growth Potential** – With **less mature ESG frameworks,** emerging markets present early-stage investment opportunities in **sustainable infrastructure and innovation,** offering the potential for **outsized returns** as these economies modernize.

Challenges of ESG Investing in Developing Economies

Despite its potential, ESG investing in emerging markets comes with notable challenges:

- **Regulatory Gaps** – Many developing economies **lack standardized ESG reporting requirements**, leading to **inconsistent and unreliable disclosures.**

- **Corporate Governance Issues** – **Weak governance structures, corruption, and transparency concerns** increase investment risks in certain regions.

- **Data Scarcity** – The availability of **accurate and timely ESG data** remains a challenge, making it difficult for investors to assess a company's sustainability performance.

Key Sectors Leading ESG in Emerging Markets

Several industries are driving ESG progress in developing economies:

- **Renewable Energy** – Countries such as **India and China** are rapidly expanding their **solar and wind energy** capacity, reducing carbon emissions and enhancing **energy security.**

- **Microfinance and Fintech** – In regions like **Africa and Southeast Asia**, microfinance institutions and fintech startups are advancing **financial inclusion and social empowerment**, delivering **impactful ESG outcomes** at the grassroots level.

- **Sustainable Agriculture** – Nations with **rich natural resources**, such as **Brazil and Indonesia**, are beginning to adopt **sustainable agricultural practices** to combat deforestation and promote biodiversity.

Investor Takeaways: Navigating ESG Risks in High-Growth Markets

To capitalize on **ESG opportunities in emerging markets**, investors should adopt a **strategic and risk-aware approach:**

1. **Conduct Rigorous Due Diligence** – Given the **lack of standardized ESG data**, independent research and **local expertise** are essential.

2. **Focus on Long-Term Impact** – Prioritize investments that contribute to **sustainable development, social progress, and economic resilience.**

3. **Diversify Across Regions and Sectors** – Spread the risk by investing in a **mix of renewable energy, fintech, and sustainable agriculture projects.**

4. **Engage Locally** – Collaborate with **local partners and stakeholders** to navigate regulatory frameworks and cultural nuances.

5. **Monitor Regulatory Developments** – Stay informed about **evolving ESG regulations**, as new disclosure standards can significantly **reshape investment landscapes.**

Author's Perspective on ESG in Emerging Markets

Emerging markets are the **next frontier** for ESG investing, offering both **significant challenges and transformative opportunities**. Although **regulatory, governance, and data hurdles persist**, the potential for **sustainable economic growth is immense.**

Investors who **conduct thorough research, engage with local contexts, and adopt a long-term perspective** can uncover hidden opportunities that **deliver both financial returns and meaningful social and environmental impact**. As these markets mature, the **integration of robust ESG practices will be key to economic stability and long-term value creation.**

CHAPTER 9

The Future of ESG—What Comes Next?

Introduction: Navigating the Next Phase of ESG Investing

As ESG investing matures, the landscape is poised for **transformative change**. The next phase will be defined by **stricter regulations, enhanced transparency, technological innovations, and new financial instruments.**

Will ESG Investing Become Mandatory?

- **Regulatory Momentum** – Governments and regulatory bodies worldwide increasingly recognize the **importance of sustainable business practices.** Many are moving toward **mandatory ESG disclosures** to ensure corporate transparency and accountability.

- **Global Alignment** – Organizations such as the **International Sustainability Standards Board (ISSB)** are pushing for **standardized ESG criteria**, aiming to reduce **greenwashing and improve comparability** across markets.

- **Implications for Investors** – Mandated ESG reporting would enhance **data quality and reliability**, enabling better-informed investment decisions. However, it may also lead to **higher compliance costs** for companies.

The Rise of AI and Big Data in ESG Analysis

- **Data-Driven Insights** – **AI and big data** are revolutionizing ESG analysis by processing vast amounts of **unstructured information**—from **social media sentiment to real-time environmental data**—to provide more accurate assessments.

- **Enhanced Transparency** – AI-powered tools allow for **continuous ESG monitoring**, reducing reliance on **self-reported data and traditional third-party ratings**.

- **Case Study** – A leading asset manager integrated an **AI-driven ESG platform** to track portfolio sustainability. By analyzing **satellite imagery, social media feeds, and corporate disclosures**, the firm identified ESG risks that traditional ratings had **overlooked**, enabling real-time adjustments.

Green Finance: The Surge of Sustainable Bonds and Impact-Driven Investments

- **The Rise of Green Bonds** – Green bonds finance **renewable energy projects, sustainable infrastructure, and conservation efforts**, offering both **financial returns and measurable environmental impact**.

- **Impact-Driven Investments** – Beyond bonds, **impact investing** is evolving, focusing on **tangible ESG outcomes**—such as **climate action, gender equality, and social equity**.

- **Investor Takeaway** – The **expanding green finance market** not only diversifies investment opportunities but also **directs capital toward global sustainability goals**.

Author's Perspective: The Road Ahead for ESG Investing

The future of ESG investing will be shaped by:

- **Stricter regulatory standards** driving transparency and accountability.

- **Technological advancements** making ESG analysis more **data-driven and precise.**

- **Innovative financial instruments** funneling capital into projects with **real-world impact.**

As ESG **evolves from a niche strategy to a fundamental pillar of modern finance**, investors who **stay informed and adaptable** will be best positioned to seize emerging opportunities.

CHAPTER 10

ESG Investment Case Studies—Successes and Failures

Introduction: Learning from Real-World Examples

Case studies provide **valuable insights** into the **practical challenges and successes** of ESG investing. This chapter examines companies that have **navigated the ESG landscape—** some successfully, others with significant missteps.

Tesla: An ESG Paradox

- **The Success Story** – Tesla **revolutionized the auto industry** with its **electric vehicles**, significantly reducing carbon emissions and challenging fossil fuel dependence.

- **The Controversy** – Despite its environmental achievements, Tesla has faced criticism over **workplace safety, labor conditions, and governance.** ESG rating agencies have penalized Tesla for these factors, illustrating **the complexity of ESG evaluation.**

- **Investor Takeaway** – Tesla's case underscores the importance of **assessing the full ESG spectrum—** strong environmental performance must be balanced by **sound governance and social responsibility.**

Unilever: A True Sustainability Leader or Just Effective Branding?

- **The Positive Side** – Unilever is widely praised for **sustainability initiatives**, including **reducing** plastic waste, ethical sourcing, and community engagement.

- **The Criticisms** – Some argue that Unilever's initiatives, while extensive, at times **serve as branding exercises rather than transformative changes**. Issues remain in **water usage and labor practices** in certain regions.

- **Investor Takeaway** – Unilever's case highlights the need for **continuous, measurable ESG improvements** rather than **relying solely on public perception**.

Wirecard: A Governance Failure Disguised as ESG Excellence

- **The Rise** – Wirecard was once regarded as a **fintech innovator** with promising ESG credentials, lauded for **transparency and technological advancement**.

- **The Fall** – The company's **collapse due to massive accounting fraud** exposed the risks of **weak governance and regulatory oversight**, despite its strong ESG branding.

- **Investor Takeaway** – The Wirecard scandal highlights the **critical importance of corporate governance**. A company's **ESG profile must be backed by sound financial and operational fundamentals**.

Key Investor Takeaways from ESG Case Studies

- **Holistic Analysis** – Assess **all ESG factors**, not just **headline ratings**.

- **Continuous Due Diligence** – Regularly **reassess companies** as ESG performance evolves.

- **Balance Ideals with Practicality** – ESG investments should **deliver financial value alongside ethical impact**.

- **Learn from Failures** – Cases like Wirecard demonstrate that **robust governance is essential.**

- **Embrace AI and Big Data** – Use **technological tools** for real-time ESG insights.

Author's Take: Lessons for the ESG Investor

Successful ESG investing requires a **balanced, data-driven approach.** Investors must:

- Look beyond marketing claims.

- Validate ESG credentials with hard data.

- Remain vigilant against potential risks.

By **learning from both successes and failures,** investors can build **resilient portfolios** that **achieve financial objectives while driving meaningful change.**

CHAPTER 11

ESG—A Passing Trend or the Future of Finance?

Introduction: The Debate on ESG's Longevity

As ESG investing continues to grow, the question remains: Is ESG a **fundamental shift** in finance, or just **a rebranded investment strategy?**

Common Misconceptions About ESG Investing

- **"ESG is just a marketing gimmick."** While **some** companies exploit ESG **branding,** many are genuinely transforming their business models.

- **"ESG guarantees higher returns."** In reality, ESG **manages long-term risk** rather than ensuring short-term outperformance.

- **"ESG is only about the environment."** ESG also includes **social and governance factors,** such as **labor practices and corporate ethics.**

- **"All ESG funds are the same."** Due to **a lack of standardization,** investors must **carefully analyze fund methodologies.**

The Real Value of ESG: Moving Beyond Compliance

- **Risk Management & Resilience** – ESG **reduces exposure** to regulatory, environmental, and reputational risks.

- **Long-Term Value Creation** – Sustainable businesses **outperform** in stability and innovation.

- **Competitive Advantage** – ESG **drives innovation** in clean energy, ethical supply chains, and corporate responsibility.

- **Global Alignment** – Companies with **strong ESG foundations** are better positioned for **future regulatory and consumer trends.**

The Road Ahead for ESG Investors

- **Standardization of ESG Reporting** – Stricter regulations will enhance **data reliability.**

- **Tech-Driven Transparency** – AI and **blockchain innovations** will improve **real-time ESG tracking.**

- **Impact-Driven Investing** – The focus will shift to **tangible, measurable ESG outcomes.**

Final Thoughts: The Future of ESG Investing

ESG is **not a passing trend**—it is **an evolving financial framework.** Investors must:

- **Look beyond ESG labels** and demand **data-backed accountability.**

- **Adapt to new technologies** that enhance ESG transparency.

- **Use ESG as a strategic tool** for long-term portfolio resilience.

The **ESG revolution is well underway.** The real question is: **Will you be part of it?**

Bonus: ESG Cheat Sheet and Must-Know Resources

Navigating the complex world of ESG investing requires **reliable tools, expert insights, and a critical approach.** This cheat sheet provides a **comprehensive guide** to evaluating ESG opportunities, distinguishing genuine sustainability efforts from **greenwashing**, and staying ahead in this rapidly evolving field.

Checklist: 5 Critical Questions to Ask Before Investing in an ESG Fund

Before committing to an ESG fund, ask yourself:

1. **What methodology does the fund use to assess ESG performance?**

    - Understanding the rating process helps avoid funds that rely on **superficial metrics or unverified claims.**

2. **How transparent is the fund's ESG data and reporting?**

    - Look for **detailed, verifiable disclosures** rather than vague marketing promises.

3. **Does the fund prioritize impact or mere compliance?**

    - True ESG leaders integrate sustainability into their **core business operations**, not just as a regulatory checkbox.

4. **What are the fund's top holdings?**

    - Ensure the fund is not heavily invested in sectors with **poor ESG track records**, such as fossil fuels or fast fashion.

5. **How has the fund performed relative to traditional benchmarks?**

    • Evaluate whether the fund's **risk-adjusted returns** align with both your **ethical standards and financial goals.**

Best ESG Data Sources for Reliable Insights

Avoid marketing hype by relying on **credible, independent** ESG data sources:

• **MSCI ESG Ratings** – A widely used scoring system evaluating corporate sustainability performance.

• **Sustainalytics** – Provides **risk-based ESG research** and **comprehensive company ratings**.

• **CDP (Carbon Disclosure Project)** – A global platform tracking **corporate carbon footprints and environmental impact.**

• **GRESB (Global Real Estate Sustainability Benchmark)** – Assesses **ESG performance in real estate and infrastructure.**

• **Morningstar ESG Research** – Offers **in-depth ESG fund analysis and sustainability ratings.**

Top Books, Podcasts, and Reports for ESG Investors

Expand your ESG knowledge with **expert-recommended** resources:

Books

• *The Sustainable Economy* – Robert S. Kaplan – How ESG factors are reshaping business and finance.

• *ESG Investing for Dummies* – Brendan Bradley – A beginner-friendly guide to ESG principles.

- *Net Positive* – Paul Polman & Andrew Winston – A roadmap for companies aiming for real ESG impact.

Podcasts

- **Sustainable Finance Podcast** – Covers **trends, regulatory changes, and investment strategies.**
- **ESG Insider by S&P Global** – Insights on **market developments and corporate sustainability efforts.**
- **The Green Investor** – Focuses on **practical ESG investment strategies and emerging trends.**

Reports

- **World Economic Forum's Global Risks Report** – Analysis of **global ESG risks and challenges.**
- **UN PRI Reports** – Research on **responsible investment practices and ESG integration.**
- **OECD Sustainable Finance Reports** – Regulatory developments and policy insights in ESG finance.

Your ESG Journey Starts Now:

Successful ESG investing requires –

- Continuous learning
- Critical analysis
- Adaptability to evolving regulations and trends

Use this **cheat sheet and expert resources** to refine your strategy, make well-informed decisions, and stay ahead in **sustainable finance.**

Bibliography

Books and Reports:

- Eccles, Robert G., and Klimenko, Svetlana. *The Investor Revolution: Shareholders Are Getting Serious About Sustainability.* Harvard Business Review, 2019.

- Friedman, Milton. *Capitalism and Freedom.* University of Chicago Press, 1962.

- Giese, Guido, et al. *Foundations of ESG Investing: How ESG Affects Equity Valuation, Risk, and Performance.* MSCI Research, 2019.

- Rifkin, Jeremy. *The Green New Deal: Why the Fossil Fuel Civilization Will Collapse, and the Bold Economic Plan to Save Life on Earth.* St. Martin's Press, 2019.

- United Nations. *Principles for Responsible Investment (UN PRI) Reports.*

- Friede, Gunnar, Busch, Timo, and Bassen, Alexander. "ESG and Financial Performance: Aggregated Evidence from More than 2000 Empirical Studies." *Journal of Sustainable Finance & Investment,* 2015.

- Kotsantonis, Sakis, Pinney, George, and Serafeim, George. "ESG Integration in Investment Management: Myths and Realities." *Journal of Applied Corporate Finance,* 2016.

- Sullivan, Robert, and Mackenzie, Mark. *Responsible Investment: Guide to ESG Data Providers and Relevant Trends.* CFA Institute, 2020.

Online Resources:

- **CDP (Carbon Disclosure Project)** – www.cdp.net

- **MSCI ESG Ratings** – www.msci.com/our-solutions/esg-investing

- **Sustainalytics** – www.sustainalytics.com

- **Global Reporting Initiative (GRI)** – www.globalreporting.org

- **World Economic Forum** – www.weforum.org

- **OECD Sustainable Finance Reports** – www.oecd.org

- **Refinitiv ESG** – www.refinitiv.com/en/sustainable-finance/esg-scores

- **Bloomberg Sustainable Finance** – www.bloomberg.com/green

- **UN PRI** – www.unpri.org

- **World Resources Institute (WRI)** – www.wri.org